Made in United States
Troutdale, OR
12/18/2024

26796242R00070